D1517335

DIANA

The People's Princess

DIANA

The People's Princess

by David J. Darling

DILLON PRESS, INC. MINNEAPOLIS, MINNESOTA

The photographs are reproduced through the courtesy of Consolidated Newspictures (AFP photos found on pp. 35, 38, 39, 44, 46, and 48) and UPI/Bettmann Archive.

Library of Congress Cataloging in Publication Data

Darling, David J.
    Diana, the people's princess.

    (Taking Part)
    SUMMARY: A brief illustrated biography of the Princess of Wales.
1. Diana, Princess of Wales, 1961-   —Juvenile literature. 2 Great
Britain—Princess and princesses—Biography—Juvenile literature.
[1. Diana, Princess of Wales, 1961-
2. Princesses] I. Title
DA591.A45D5313   1984   941.085′092′4   [92]   84-12687

ISBN 0-87518-282-8 (lib. bdg.)

Dillon Press, Inc., 242 Portland Avenue South
Minneapolis, Minnesota 55415

Printed in the United States of America

        3 4 5 6 7 8 9 10 91 90 89 88 87 86

Contents

Diana, Princess of Wales

Few people had heard of Lady Diana Spencer before Prince Charles began dating her in July 1980. Two months later, newspapers around the world named her, "Prince Charles's new girlfriend." But even then Lady Diana was given little public attention.

As the relationship between Charles and Diana deepened, so did the public's interest. When her engagement to Prince Charles became official, Lady Diana's name became known throughout the world, and her life would never again be quite the same.

Diana Frances Spencer was just twenty years old when she married Prince Charles and became the princess of Wales. Less than a year later, she had not only won the hearts of the British people, but she had given them a male heir to the British throne. Touching people with her warmth, charm, and caring attitude, she was, from the beginning, the people's princess.

Diana's story is one mixed with luxury and security, happy times and sad, country mansions and London flats, private schools and royal activities. But it is Diana, herself, who shines beyond her dazzling background and lifestyle. Her strong will and determination, mixed with her shyness and charm, give her enormous popularity with the British people, who openly show deep affection for their future queen.

1/A Carefree Country Childhood

People everywhere called the event the "wedding of the century." The day was a mixture of magic and majesty when Charles, Prince of Wales, married Lady Diana Spencer. Around the world millions of people watched the wedding on television. Throughout Great Britain church bells rang, and in the streets of London the people cheered and waved their union jacks. At last their prince had chosen England's future queen.

Even for Charles, heir to the throne of England, the size of such a celebration was rather special. But to his young bride, the royal event was new and exciting, and just a little frightening.

Since her romance with Charles became known, Lady Diana Spencer had quite suddenly become one of the most famous, most talked-about women in the world. Everywhere she went, she was photographed. Yet, only months earlier, few people even knew her name.

Diana was born on July 1, 1961, during one of the hottest summer afternoons anyone in England could remember. Her father, Edward John Spencer, who at that time was Viscount Althorp, and her mother, Frances, already had two daughters, Sarah, aged six, and Jane, aged four. Now they wanted a son, who would someday receive his father's title and great wealth. The parents, however, would have to wait longer for a son.

From the moment of her birth, Diana began life as she would continue it—doing things her own way! Any disappointment her parents might have felt about having another daughter quickly turned to joy. "She was a delightful child," her father recalled, "and as a baby she could have won any beauty competition."

Healthy, happy, Diana was also far from being ordinary. Her family was a most noble one, and she herself had a title—the Honorable Diana Frances Spencer. Her home was Park House, a comfortable mansion on the huge Sandringham estate in Norfolk. The Spencer's property was only a few hundred yards from one of the queen's own country houses. Strange though it would seem to most children, at Park House Diana had a nanny, Judith, to help look after her.

As a baby, Diana was given lots of attention. Her sisters would bathe her, dress her, and brush her hair, as if she were a live doll. Together they would go for a walk with Judith or Mother in the beautiful grounds of Park House.

Like her sisters, Diana was taught strictly, but fondly, how to behave as a member of a noble family. She was expected to follow certain rules. Never be noisy. Never interrupt or speak with your mouth full. Sit up straight at the table, smile, and be polite. Always keep your room tidy!

In May 1964, when Diana was nearly three, her little brother, Charles, was born. At last, a boy! When Charles was christened shortly afterwards in the splendor of Westminster Abbey, his youngest sister missed the grand event. Diana had tumbled down a flight of steps the day before and bruised her head quite badly.

When she was four, Diana began lessons with the family governess, Miss Gertrude Allen. Painting, gluing, and cutting were some of Diana's activities. She did all those wonderfully messy things that four year olds love. Miss Allen remembers that, even then, she was "a tidy soul" and always "a real trier." Still, there must have been times when "Ally" wasn't looking that Diana's attention turned from her work to the view through the tall sash windows. As she watched the trees and the grazing cattle in the park outside, did she ever dream of becoming a princess?

Diana was certainly no stranger to royalty. Her father had worked for the queen for many years, and the two families knew each other well. Both her sisters and her brother had royal godparents, although Diana did not. When the queen and her family stayed at the big house at Sandringham, the royal children and the young Spencers would often play together.

A great attraction at Park House was the heated, outdoor swimming pool. Diana's father had had the pool built, and the children thought it was wonderful. Complete with diving board and slide, the pool was the only one for miles around. Here Diana would swim and splash for hours in the company of her sisters and the young princes, Edward and Andrew.

Sometimes after school Diana would go shopping with her mother in the nearby village of Snettisham. Once in a while there would be a longer trip to King's Lynn. On other occasions, Diana would visit her father's farm to see the newborn calves.

In the summer there was the greatest treat of all. The family owned a small cabin at Brancaster, a seaside village on the north coast of Norfolk, only a twenty-minute drive from Park House. On weekends when the weather was pleasant, the Spencers would go there for a picnic. Often the entire day would be spent playing in the sea or among the sand dunes.

Summer was Diana's favorite time of year. There was swimmming and more swimming! She also enjoyed climbing the beech trees at the front of the house and bicycling along the gravel drives.

Lots of pets could be found at Park House, especially horses, dogs (spaniels), and hamsters. One of the Spencer pets was Romany, a rather bad-tempered pony owned by Diana's sisters.

There were also friends to play with. Sometimes Diana's playmates were royal friends—Prince Edward and Prince Andrew. The queen and her family, however, only stayed at Sandringham a few weeks each year. More often, Diana would play with Penelope Ashton, the rector's daughter, or Alexandra Lloyd, another neighbor on the estate.

Those early years at Park House were among the happiest, most carefree of Diana's life. She loved the old place, which was always warm and friendly. Outside the mansion, the grounds must have been a delightful garden for her. Little did Diana realize that her strength and courage would soon be tested.

2/Growing Up

In the fall of 1967, a change took place in the Spencer home, which darkened Diana's safe and happy life. Shortly after Diana's sixth birthday, her mother and father separated. Although the Spencers were good parents, their marriage had not been a happy one. Now Frances, Diana's mother, felt she must go and begin a new life in another place.

At about the same time, Sarah and Jane were sent to boarding school. Park House was suddenly empty and quiet. Yet little Diana, helped by her father and grandmothers, faced the change bravely. Young as she was, she already had the strong will and tough character that would serve her well in the years to come.

Diana was a remarkably tidy girl. Everything she owned was arranged neatly on shelves or in cupboards in her bedroom. She loved soft toys. Her father remembers,

"She loved her soft toys nearly as much as she loved babies. She always loved babies."

With Frances gone, Diana poured even more energy into the things she did. Chattering from morning till night, she never allowed herself time to think about missing Mummy. She played for hours with her young brother, fussing over him like a mother hen.

In January the decision was made that both Diana and Charles should start day school. Going to school was a big change from private lessons with Ally in the downstairs room. But Silfield, in King's Lynn, was a small, family school. In these surroundings, the two young Spencers quickly learned to fit in with the other children.

In school Diana was well mannered, showed good sense, and had a keen interest in her brother's nursery class. She was very fond of young children and enjoyed working with them in all types of activities.

During holidays, Diana would spend time with each of her parents. Visiting Mother now meant a train ride to London. On one of these visits, Diana learned that her mother had fallen in love with Peter Shand Kydd, a wealthy businessman. The couple would soon marry.

Back at Park House, Father had a special treat planned for Diana's seventh birthday. He had made a secret arrangement with the local zoo. As the party guests arrived, they were asked to form a line. When everyone was ready, across the lawn came Bert the camel, led by his keeper. Much to their delight, everyone was given a camel ride.

Viscount Althorp was always kind to his children. Having a large farm to manage, however, kept him very busy. He soon decided that it would be best for Diana to go away to boarding school.

Just like her sisters, Sarah and Jane, Diana was sent to Riddlesworth Hall. This school for girls was a beautiful, large, sandstone mansion. Set in acres of wooded countryside, Riddlesworth was a two-hour drive from Park House. The school was run in a firm but friendly way by Miss Elizabeth Ridsdale, known as "Riddy." Each day began at 7:30 sharp with the ringing of an old cowbell. This sound was the signal for the girls to tumble out of bed. Girls with long hair then formed a line to have their hair put in braids, or plaits. How Diana hated the rubber bands! Breakfast was at 8:00. After the girls had eaten, beds had to be made and prayers said in the senior common room. When these things were done, classes finally began.

A special part of the school was Pet's Corner. All the girls were encouraged to bring a small pet as a helpful cure for homesickness. Diana's personal pride and joy was a guinea pig named Peanuts. As her mother would say, she was fond "of anything in a small cage."

Over the next few years, Diana was seen as cheerful, lighthearted, and even tempered. Riddy remembered, "She was always a decent, kind, and happy little girl. Everyone seemed to like her . . . . What stands out in my mind is how awfully sweet she was with the little ones."

Diana's interests were clear. She cared a great deal for young children and had a concern for their well-being. She also enjoyed sports: swimming, tennis, and netball, which is a game like basketball. Dancing was also a favorite activity. "I'm obsessed with ballet," she later said, "and I also love tap dancing."

Like the one hundred and twenty other girls at Riddlesworth Hall, Diana enjoyed weekends the best. Only on weekends after lunch were the girls allowed candies

from their tuck boxes. Sunday brought more treats. On Sundays the girls could lie-in until 8:15, and breakfast included sausages. After church service, the girls were treated to roast lunch and a long walk on the heath behind the school.

When she was twelve, Diana moved to a new boarding school near Sevenoaks in Kent. West Heath was a school with all the old-fashioned, strict, but friendly rules that Riddy had taught. Girls were encouraged to "develop their own minds and tastes and to realize their duties as citizens."

Diana's tastes were not for schoolwork. Always an independent young woman, Diana preferred to read romances and watch television when she was supposed to be studying. Her tastes, instead, were towards art, music, and ballet. Later, at age sixteen like many English schoolchildren, Diana would take the important Ordinary "O" Levels, the standard British school examinations, which she failed to pass. In school studies, Diana's carefree style let her down.

Yet, in other ways, Diana was growing up to be very much like her mother, now Mrs. Shand Kydd. With the same mixture of firmness and charm, Diana was a strong-willed person, quietly able to make people do what she wanted.

As time went by, Diana seemed to enjoy the company of her mother more and more. Frances became a friend—a good, close friend—with whom Diana could talk and confide. For Diana, Frances's and Peter's new farm in Scotland was especially thrilling. Set on a wild, windy hillside on a remote island, the farm was a place straight out of a child's adventure story. Together with friends, Diana went there in the summer and helped look after her mother's Shetland ponies. Sometimes Peter would take her out in the boat to fish for mackerel or to put down lobster pots. Always the swimmer, Diana would, now and then, take an icy dip in the Atlantic Ocean.

Although the farm in Scotland was always a thrill, Park House was home to Diana. In June 1975, when her grandfather, the seventh earl Spencer, died, Diana's father received the title, eighth earl Spencer as well as Althorp estate in Northamptonshire. At the same time, Diana, along with her sisters, received the title, lady,

while her brother, Charles, became the new viscount Althorp. Obtaining the estate and new titles also meant leaving Park House.

When Diana came home to Park House that summer, the move to Althorp was already under way. Packing crates lined the hallways, and rooms echoed in emptiness, as memories of a happy childhood were carted away. The thought of leaving Park House was too upsetting for Diana. She called her girlfriend Alex Lloyd, and the two agreed to spend a last day at Brancaster, eating peaches on the beach.

Diana's new home was certainly very different. Though Park House would have seemed big to most people, Althorp Hall, the ancestral home of the Spencer family, was truly enormous. Housing one of the finest private art collections in Europe, Althorp was a vast, stately home with marble floors, chandeliers, and priceless furniture.

Diana would never grow to be fond of Althorp. As she later said, "I feel my roots are in Norfolk. I have always loved it there." Although she was upset by the move, there was for Diana, an even greater change about to take place. Shorty after moving into Althorp, Earl Spencer married Raine, the countess of Dartmouth. For the Spencer children, the marriage came like a sudden storm at sea. Diana's new stepmother, forceful and strong-willed, quickly took over the running of the family home. Sarah and Jane avoided her as much as possible. But Diana, with her cheerful manner and her own strong will, would continue to live her own life.

Earl Spencer remembered Diana, years earlier, during a rare visit to her grandfather's, "flying down the front staircase (at Althorp Hall) on a tea tray." Now in her teens, she would still fill the great, gloomy rooms of Althorp with spirit and life—even after Raine had decided that the house should be opened to the public. Setting up a record player in the splendid entrance hall, Diana would tap dance on the marble floor. In summer she would swim all day or walk around the glorious park in the most casual clothing.

Diana never allowed her wealth or position to get in her way of what she wanted to do. Though her new home, one of the finest in England, was complete with servants, Diana chose to do her own washing and ironing. Her sim-

ple bedroom was an old night nursery with two single beds and a sofa lined with her favorite soft toys.

Her room also contained a bookshelf filled with romances written by Raine's mother, Barbara Cartland, a well-known English romance novelist. Diana enjoyed love stories, yet little did she know that a love story of her very own was just around the corner. Diana's love story would be a true romance that would be watched, as well as read, by millions of people.

3/Courting a Prince

In the summer of 1977, Diana's sister Sarah began dating the Queen's eldest son, Prince Charles, heir to the English throne. They had met at the Ascot race course in June. In November, Charles went to Althorp as Sarah's guest at a shooting party. Here Charles and Diana met. "I remember thinking what a very jolly and amusing and attractive sixteen year old she was. I mean great fun—bouncy and full of life," Prince Charles would later say. Diana confessed, too, that she found him "pretty amazing."

After Christmas, Diana went to finishing school in Switzerland. For Diana, at the age of sixteen, the trip was her first time in an airplane and her first trip outside Great Britain. She hated her new adventure. Diana had had enough of schools that turned out proper, young ladies. Coming home after just six weeks, she moved into her mother's apartment at Cadogan Place in Chelsea, London.

While Diana had been away, Earl Spencer had suffered a massive brain hemorrhage. He would, perhaps, have died had it not been for the care and devotion of his second wife, Raine. With amazing energy, Raine sought out the best doctors, the best hospitals, and even a rare, new drug that might offer hope for her husband. The earl gradually recovered, and, as a result, Raine earned the respect, if not the love, of her four stepchildren.

Meanwhile, in London, life took a new turn for Diana. Offering her services as a nanny, she began doing what she enjoyed most of all—caring for children. One of her favorite children was a young American boy, Patrick, whom she looked after for more than a year.

In July 1978, Diana learned to drive a car. At first, she was not very successful. Having failed her test once, she later went on to crash the new Volkswagen that her mother had given her. Not surprisingly, she often chose to ride her bicycle through the busy London streets instead, which can also be quite frightening.

With roommates, Laura Grieg and Sophie Kimball, Diana spent most of her free time in the city doing quiet things. She enjoyed shows and movies, dining out at small cafes, or simply staying home and chatting, while watching television. The only parties she went to were with close friends. She disliked the noisy, smoky atmosphere of discos. Diana once took a cooking course and was, in fact, a good cook. Several times she provided the food at parties. Her weekends, however, were spent away from London. Diana enjoyed visits to her friends' homes in the country, to Althorp, and to Scotland.

In January 1979, an invitation came for Diana and her sister Sarah to be guests of the queen at a shooting party at Sandringham. Prince Charles was there, too. After the Sandringham shoot, Diana and Charles began to see more of each other. Charles would simply call up Cadogan Place, out of the blue, and ask to speak to Diana. He would then invite her out, along with other friends, to the ballet or the opera.

Diana was always fun to be with, and, at first, Charles simply enjoyed her company. She was someone with whom he felt at ease. Diana was also someone the reporters did not suspect of being his "latest" girlfriend.

Throughout 1979, Charles and Diana would meet

every couple of months. A closer friendship grew between them. Still, could Charles, now thirty, think of this shy, fresh-faced teenager as his future wife?

When she was eighteen, Diana persuaded Earl Spencer to buy her an expensive London flat at 60 Coleherne Court. Soon she was joined there by three old chums, Virginia Pitman, Carolyn Pride, and Anne Bolton.

Up until this time, Diana never really had a regular job. In noble families, for a woman to have a career was unusual. But in September 1979, Diana began working at the Young England Kindergarten in Pimlico. The school was only a cycle ride away from her flat on Old Brompton Road. As her mother has said, Diana was "a pied piper with children." At the kindergarten, she felt completely at home, organizing the art work for fifty toddlers. Caring for each and every child and treating them as individuals, Diana didn't mind a bit her messy chores of mixing paints, sorting sticky glue pots, or washing brushes.

While working at the kindergarten, Diana kept up her interest in dancing. For a while, she had been a student teacher at Miss Betty Vacini's Dance School in Knightsbridge. Then, in March 1979, she enrolled at the Dance

Centre, Covent Garden, for classes in tap and jazz.

Life for Diana was going along quietly and normally. There were, of course, those occasional, always unexpected phone calls from Prince Charles, followed by an exciting date at the ballet or a West End show. But little else disturbed her daily life.

4/In the Public Eye

In July 1980, there came an invitation that would change Diana's life forever. Charles would be playing polo for his team, Les Diables Bleus, in Sussex. Would Diana care to come and watch? Diana accepted the invitation, and after the polo game, the couple went dancing. Suddenly, the Prince was seeing Diana as if for the first time. No longer was she the shy, slightly awkward schoolgirl from West Heath. She had turned into a beautiful young woman —charming, graceful, and kind.

Later that month, Diana received another royal invitation. Would Lady Diana like to join Charles, together with other guests, on board the royal yacht *Britannia?* She would. Later, she would also enjoy tipping His Royal Highness's windsurfer, which sent him plunging into the chilly English Channel! Charles soon forgave Diana for the spill. A week later, two dozen red roses arrived at Coleherne Court for Diana from the Prince of Wales.

As the public became aware of Charles's continued interest in Diana, the eyes of the world began to turn toward her. In September she stayed as a guest of the royal family at Balmoral in Scotland. A clever reporter had spied Charles salmon fishing in the river nearby. But who was this young woman watching him from the bank?

Diana had her back to the reporter but could see his reflection in a small hand mirror. She decided to play a game with the unwelcome visitor. Coolly and calmly, keeping her head turned so that no one could see her face, she marched straight up a steep hill and out of sight!

For Diana, this experience with the reporter was only one of many tricks that she would soon have to play in order to shake newspeople off her tracks. Within days of the visit to Balmoral, her picture appeared in papers and magazines all around the world. "Lady Diana Spencer —Prince Charles's new girlfriend" was the message. But for the prince, who had been seen with many lovely companions in the past, could Diana become more than just another girlfriend?

Diana, princess of Wales, waves to the crowd as she leaves Saint Paul's Cathedral on July 29, 1981.

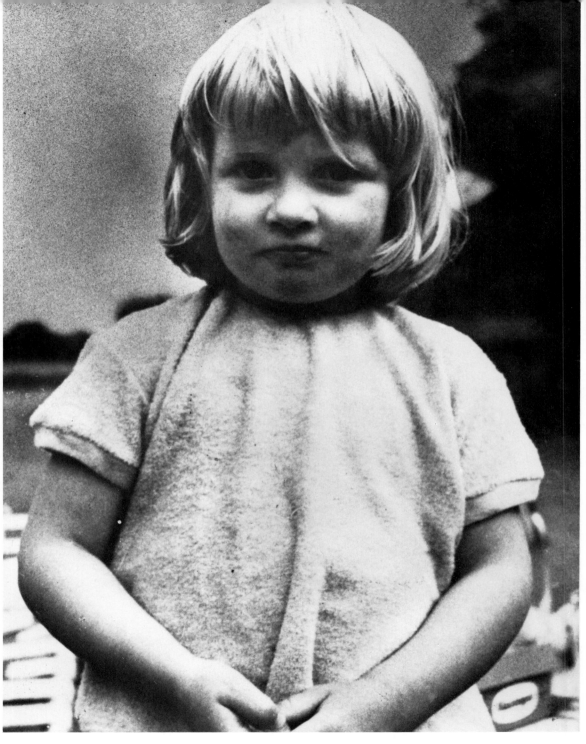

Diana (age three), at Park House, looks like an ordinary little girl.

Who would have guessed that twenty years later Diana would be a princess?

At age seven, Diana traveled to London to spend her school vacation with her mother.

In 1970, Diana (age nine) spent a summer holiday at Itchenor, in Sussex.

More than two thousand invited guests watch as the royal wedding party approach the altar in Saint Paul's Cathedral.

Standing between her father and Prince Charles, Lady Diana listens as the Archbishop of Canterbury reads the wedding service.

Following the wedding ceremony, the prince and princess greet their subjects, as their carriage makes its way through the streets of London.

On the balcony of Buckingham Palace, the bride and groom kiss.

Whether posing formally for an official portrait at the couple's home at Highgrove (left) *or casually for a television interview* (above), *Diana shows grace and charm.*

Prince William Arthur Philip Louis, born June 21, 1982, is shown with his mother (right). *He is also shown* (above), *following his christening at Buckingham Palace, with his parents, his grandparents Queen Elizabeth and Prince Philip, and his great-grandmother the Queen Mother.*

As princess of Wales, Diana devotes time to royal duties. Here she visits a factory in Ware, England.

Precious moments are the ones which catch Diana at home in Kensington Palace with Prince William.

As an ambassador for Great Britain, Diana joins Charles on a goodwill tour of Australia and New Zealand. In the Australian outback, the royal couple stand before Ayers Rock, a popular landmark.

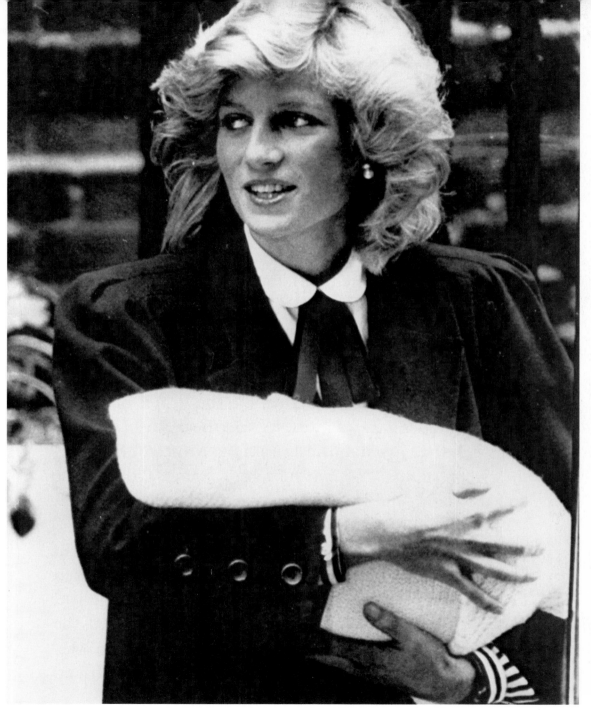

Diana leaves Saint Mary's Hospital with her new son, Henry Charles Albert David, born September 15, 1984.

The prince wouldn't be rushed into marriage. "To me, marriage seems to be the biggest and most responsible step to be taken in one's life," he had said. Furthermore, he went on, "When you marry in my position, you are going to marry someone who perhaps one day is going to be queen. You have to choose somebody very carefully, I think, who could fill this particular role."

Was Diana the right person? Her background was certainly good. Her family tree could be traced back to four kings of England. Not only did she have royal blood, but she was even a distant cousin to the Prince of Wales. Diana shared Charles's interests, too. Both loved the outdoors. Both enjoyed music and skiing. Most importantly, they were friends. "You must be good friends," the Prince had insisted, "and love, I am sure, will grow out of that friendship."

On February 5, 1981, after the couple had dinner in his rooms at Buckingham Palace, Prince Charles asked Lady Diana to marry him. Immediately, she replied, "yes." The engagement of the royal couple ended the public's curiosity as to how serious their friendship was. Diana was no longer thought of as just another girlfriend of Prince Charles. She was now recognized as the soon-to-be princess of Wales.

Diana's life would never be quite the same again. There would be no more days at the kindergarten in Pimlico. She could no longer share a flat with her girlfriends. The day after her engagement to Charles was announced, she moved into Clarence House, the London home of the Queen Mother. Here she would learn what would be expected of her as princess of Wales and how to behave in a royal manner. The next morning she awoke in a royal bedroom, and her duties as princess-to-be began.

Asked how he thought his fiancee would cope, Charles replied, "I'm sure she'll be very, very good . . . . It's obviously difficult to start with, but you just have to take the plunge."

Diana did, indeed, take the plunge. At Buckingham Palace, thousands of telegrams and letters of congratulations had arrived. Diana's first task was to start reading through her enormous amount of mail. This was only the beginning of a long list of things to be done. After all, Lady Diana had a wedding to plan—and a royal one at that!

In between making plans for the wedding, Lady Diana also attended banquets and opening ceremonies, speeches, and galas. All at once she was caught up in the nonstop whirl of royal duties. There was a dinner with the president of Nigeria, a lunch with the president of Ghana, a banquet in honor of King Khaled of Saudi Arabia, and so the list of activities went on.

During one of her many official outings, a schoolboy from the watching crowd stepped forward and handed Diana a single, yellow daffodil. "May I kiss the hand of my future queen?" he asked. "Yes, you may," Diana replied, adding with a blush, "You'll never live this down!"

Her sense of humor, her warmth, and her fresh, natural charm quickly made her a favorite of everyone. Thousands of British schoolgirls—not to mention many top models—had their hair styled to look just like "Lady Di." Her stunning clothes were copied. What Diana chose to wear today, became the fashion of tomorrow.

There was, of course, the wedding itself. Britain had not seen such happy preparations and such excitement in years. The wedding was to take place on July 29, 1981, in Saint Paul's Cathedral. Throughout the country, months before the wedding was to take place, people everywhere were displaying their love for the royal couple.

On the morning of the wedding, an unusual quiet filled the capital. No cars or buses moved along the road from the stately palace to the great cathedral. Instead, people, thousands upon thousands, stood ten deep on the sidewalk. The crowds buzzed with excitement, as they stood waiting patiently for the wedding party to pass by.

Soon the ceremonial drive to the cathedral began. Soldiers of the queen's own guard, on their high-stepping horses, rode by. Amid them were the splendid coaches that carried Queen Elizabeth, her husband Prince Philip, the royal princes and princesses, and, finally, Lady Diana. Waving to the delighted crowds, the wedding party wound its way to Saint Paul's.

As Diana stepped from the glass coach, she approached the greatest moment of her young life. Wearing a beautiful gown of white silk and lace, she entered the cathedral. Organ music filled the mighty church as over two thousand heads turned to watch the beautiful bride. With her father at her side, Lady Diana Spencer walked down the aisle to where her prince was waiting.

"Here is the stuff of which fairy tales are made," spoke the Archbishop of Canterbury, "the prince and princess on their wedding day. But fairy tales usually end at this point...Our faith sees the wedding day, not as the place of arrival, but the place where the adventure really begins."

Repeating their marriage promises, Charles and Diana began their adventure together. A great cheer rose from the crowd outside, flags waved, and smiles broke out on the faces of a million waiting people, as the royal couple left the cathedral.

From Saint Paul's, the prince and princess were cheered through a sea of happy, loyal Britons back to Buckingham Palace. Four times they appeared on the balcony overlooking the happy crowds beyond the palace gates. Finally, with Prince Andrew egging them on, to everyone's delight, the happy couple shyly kissed.

A few days of quiet rest at Broadlands was followed by a three-week honeymoon cruise in the Mediterranean aboard the royal yacht. On their return, Diana was asked what she thought of married life so far. "I can highly recommend it!" she replied.

For the young princess, life was now far different than

it had been only a year earlier. Then, she was a teenage helper at a local kindergarten. Her home was a London flat shared with three other young women. Now, she was the future queen of England.

5/The People's Princess

There was no doubt, from the moment she emerged from Saint Paul's Cathedral, that Diana was the "people's princess." Charles was quick to realize it, too. "I'm sorry, there's only one of her," he was later heard to say. "I haven't got enough wives to go around!"

Wherever she went, Diana captured the attention and the imagination of everyone. In Wales, three months after her wedding, she made her first official royal tour with Charles. Although rain, and more rain, tumbled from the gray October sky, thousands of people came out to greet her. For Diana, the Welsh people smiled and cheered and proudly waved their Welsh dragon flags.

In early December, Diana visited a school near her new home at Highgrove House in Gloucestershire. The pupils of Saint Mary's Junior School, Tetbury, were overjoyed. They had never really expected the princess to accept their invitation, which had been sent out before the royal wedding. But Diana always made time to be with children, or the elderly, or the sick. For over two hours she chatted with the pupils, laughed, and sang carols.

Christmas for Diana and Charles that year was even more exciting than usual. The announcement had been made, only a month earlier, that the Princess was expecting her first child. All of Great Britain cheered the happy news. Britons awaited the birth with the same enthusiasm they had displayed for the royal wedding.

The princess gave birth to a boy on the evening of June 21, 1982. The royal baby was the first future king born in a public hospital, Saint Mary's in Paddington, and the first heir to the English throne to have his father present at his birth. Healthy, with fair hair and blue eyes, he was christened William Arthur Philip Louis at Buckingham Palace on August 4.

Like all royal ch:'dren, Prince William would have a nanny. But Diana was determined to be with him whenever possible. She wanted her family to remain close-knit. Prince William's birth presented new challenges for her. Again, her strong will was tested. As much as she wanted to put her child first, often royal duties called her away.

As a wife, Diana has also shown her firmness and charm. People have already noted how she has changed Charles's life since their marriage. He appears more calm and more understanding of others. In Diana, Charles has found an equal in strength of will and determination.

Though thirteen years separates them in age, the prince and princess have a happy and closely shared private life. Their common interests in music, the outdoors, and children are shared wholeheartedly. Quiet moments together are treasured, and busier times are accepted without complaint.

In March 1983, Diana, Charles, and their young son left for a grand tour of Australia and New Zealand. Once again, the crowds flocked to see the tall, gracious princess with the heartwarming smile. In Brisbane alone, 130,000 people gathered to greet the royal family. From the magnificent opera house at Sydney to the mysterious Ayers Rock of the Australian outback, Diana was never far from the watching eyes of sightseers and photographers.

In June, Charles and Diana traveled to Canada for a briefer, but no less hectic, tour. On this visit, Canadian

Indians sporting their colorful, feathered headdresses greeted the prince and princess, who had sadly left Prince William in England.

In Edmonton, Charles opened the World University Games. But again Diana stole the show, casting her own special magic on the people who filled the city's streets. Every place Diana visited the response was the same. The princess had a wonderful, natural talent for making all those she met feel very happy and special.

On July 1, Diana celebrated her twenty-second birthday with 850 other guests at a Klondike Party in Fort Edmonton, Alberta, Canada. A barbecue and old-time singing were the attractions. To everyone's enjoyment, Charles, dressed in an 1860s-style frock coat and suit, and Diana, in a Victorian bustle and bow-trimmed bonnet, linked arms with the other guests and sang music hall favorites.

The royal summer filled with tours of Australia, New Zealand, and Canada had been a huge success. From it all, Diana was seen as a shining ambassador for her country. Who could doubt her ability to be a good future queen?

Photographed and interviewed everywhere she goes, Diana has stirred up a new interest in the British monarchy. She is not afraid to reach out and warm the hands of a shivering child in the crowd. She will stop at the corner store to buy candy if she feels like it. She shows, in every way, that she is warm, caring, and kind. For all these reasons, she is loved by the Britons and well-liked throughout the world.

Since she has become princess of Wales, Diana has given much to her country through her work and travels. As a mother, she has given England a king for the next century. Now, the royal couple have celebrated the birth of their second child. Henry Charles Albert David was born on September 15, 1984.

In the years ahead, Diana's life will include endless daily tasks as wife, mother, and queen-to-be. There may be times when her great adventure seems more like a weary chore. But Diana's charm and strength of character will keep her true to herself and true to everything in which she believes. She is, and will remain, the people's princess.

 *Glossary*

ambassador—a person sent to a foreign country as a chief representative of his/her own government or ruler

ancestral—coming from or belonging to a family line

Britons—natives of Great Britain

countess—the title given to the wife of an earl; or a woman who, herself, holds the rank of earl

disco—a nightclub for dancing to live and recorded music

earl—in Great Britain, the name given to a member of a specific group of people who has inherited or has been given a British title

estate—a person's property in land, usually with a large house on it

flat—an apartment on one floor

heath—a tract of unused land, usually unsuitable for growing

lie-in—to sleep in; to sleep late on purpose

monarchy—a government ruled by a single person who inherits and holds the position for life

noble—of or belonging to a class of titled persons whose rank is above all other people

ordinary levels—the first level of standard British school examinations taken by most children in Great Britain when they are sixteen years old

polo—a popular game in Great Britain, played by teams of players on horseback, using mallets with long handles to drive a wooden ball

roast lunch—a big three-course meal with roast meat, potatoes, and vegetables

shire—the name given to a county in England; for example, Northampton*shire* means the county of Northampton

tuck box—a container for food, especially sweets and pastry

viscount—a title given to a man of noble rank, which is below an earl

INDEX

The Author

Born and raised in Great Britain, David Darling is a contemporary of Prince Charles and an admirer of the royal family. Having grown up in the same era as the future heir to the British throne, Darling also shares the prince's fascination with Diana.

Working from his home in the north of England, David Darling has written numerous articles and books for young people. He holds a Ph.D. from the University of Manchester in England and enjoys giving astronomy talks in local schools.

Mr. Darling currently lives in Kirkoswald with his wife and two children.